Praise for
SOAR READY:
Medicine Poems for a Changing World:

"*Soar Ready* begins with the poet donning bird feathers and the assurance that shadows are her friends. Indeed, Szarek both takes flight and descends into the shadows of her country and her own past. The reader comes away from the book feeling embraced by her words, trusting the writer's kindness, and soaring through the compassion and spirit she creates with verse."

–KIKA DORSEY,
Author: *"Rust"* and *"Coming up for Air"*

"These poems are not merely words written on a page. They are, rather, sacred revelations of one woman's journey to find her authentic self. It is as if she kneels at the altar of art and beseeches the Muse to give her energy and craft to serve. This volume is testimony that her wish has been granted."

–DOROTHY WALTERS, PH.D.,
Author: *"Kundalini Wonder: the god/goddess in Your Body"*;
"Some Kiss We Want"; and *"The Kundalini Poems"*

"Valerie A Szarek is a joyful survivor, keen observer of nature, a wise woman and a Shaman—in short, a healer of the first order. With echoes of Mary Oliver, her poems capture a journey that places her within a community of spirits, animals, people, and nature that is embracing and nurturing."

–LORRIE WOLFE,
Author: *"Holding: From Shtetl to Santa"* and President of
Columbine State Poetry Society Northern Chapter

"Szarek has a compassionate way of shredding illusion and finding value in the hard truths of reality, a way of finding gems in the gravel and beauty in the grit. Life has taught her to appreciate the gifts given, accept mistakes made, and understand that love is all that matters in the end."

–M.D. Friedman,
Executive Editor of Liquid Light Press

"Every Poem is a Love Poem"

–Julie Cummings,
President, National Federation of State Poetry Societies,
author of *"Ride of My Life"*

SOAR READY

*Medicine Poems
for a Changing World*

SOAR READY

*Medicine Poems
for a Changing World*

Valerie A. Szarek

LAUGHING TURTLE PRESS
Louisville, Colorado

Soar Ready: Medicine Poems for a Changing World

Copyright © 2020 Valerie A Szarek

ISBN: 978-1-7352330-0-0

Publisher: Laughing Turtle Press
(Subsidiary: Breezy Mountain Press)
Louisville, Colorado

All rights reserved. No part of this book may be copied
or reproduced in any form without written permission from
the author except for brief passages quoted in reviews in newspaper, press, or online, with proper acknowledgement.

Permission is granted to educators to create copies of
individual poems for use in the classroom or workshops
with proper acknowledgement and credits.

poetval.com
Contact: val@poetval.com

Printed in the Unites States of America
Book Design: Robert Schram, Bookends Design

WELCOME

FROM THE CALM BEFORE a Presidential election year to the destructive aftermath that has followed...

From COVID 19 to the dumpster fires of civil unrest, our own military ordered into the streets with bayonets and tanks...

From the time I capitalized President to using a mere number to name; my eraser at the ready...

From when I wrote the medicines of power and intentions for the progress of our expanding hearts to now...when we need them to survive a pleading planet...

This book has traveled and gathered medicines and been birthed. She is oriented within a span of time, bookends to a collection of necessary poems. My Shamanic writing/journeys have shown me ways to create and maintain sanity and this book carries much of what I have learned.

I invite you to enter liminal space and toss aside the bounds of time. This is an invitation to play and breathe and feel and grieve. And come back. To sanity. We need you here. We are in a revolution and it is from the inside, out. Let this book assist you to open up a little wider and to discover...everything. Especially your own beauty, power and magic.

Welcome home. I'm so glad you're here! Thank you for reading and supporting my work in this world.

poetval.com
val@poetval.com

CONTENTS

Soar Ready 🐦 1
5 small 🐦 3
Indigenous 🐦 4
Dear Congress 🐦 7
May our Poems 🐦 10
Wage Sanity 🐦 12
Dear America 🐦 14
These Colors Don't Run 🐦 16
Bomb 'em with butter 🐦 19
Letter to COVID 19 🐦 21
A pandemic with Felix 🐦 23
Channeling Dr Seuss in a Quarantine 🐦 24
ode to an eraser 🐦 26
Blue 🐦 28
Letters to an Unknown God 🐦 30
autographed by fire 🐦 33
The best poem I've written 🐦 35
39 years ago I died 🐦 38
Guardian Angel 🐦 40
to heroin addiction 🐦 41
Catalpa Tree/Sister 🐦 42
Demons, again 🐦 44
No Legacy 🐦 45
Shine 🐦 46
Resilience 🐦 48
A Hallelujah (of waves) 🐦 49
Appropriate 🐦 50
When to write a Prose Poem 🐦 54
reluctant power animal 🐦 55

untolled 56
Ring 58
Touch 60
7 Degrees 62
In the Shape of Mourning 64
This Winter's Day 66
The Journey 68
Sky Bled Red 70
For Jim (the man of) Steele 72
what isn't in your poem 75
Don't stay home 76
There's no Place 78
how to write an erotic poem
(in a crowded coffee shop) 79
Never before written 83
Heckle/Jeckle 86
crow courage 88
High Water Sonata 90
Dark Moon 92
I open my window 94
Autumn 95
Related 97
Christmas Cactus 98
Still Point (Winter Solstice) 99
My stone bear closed one eye this December 100
Amazing Grace Revisited 103
8 days 104
Remember me this way 105
Obituary for a Poet 107

Soar Ready

I had my feathers
replaced
today

along my shoulders
and the
back of my neck

the old ones hardly
catching
the currents anymore

I'd forgotten to molt

and hung onto
everything
I'd ever had

today I let go-
plucked the disheveled
and replaced them with the grand

part angel, part great blue heron
and downy-owl feathers
along my spine

I don the taloned feet of hawk
firm, relaxed
unfettered by storms

I see the moon
differently

shadows
as friends

5 small

people gift

   little notebooks

      to writers

         a recipe for

            claustrophobia

               prison to

                  a sentence

                     too beautiful

                      to sully

                         5 small notebooks

                            on a shelf

                               their possibilities

                                   more interesting

                                     than words

Indigenous

I'm an original
born to this land
my first blood
watered the native Michigan rivers

red cardinal song
my after birth
seeded Flaming aboriginal Maple trees

I left my rubber soles
by that particular road
and carried a pine wood flute
to the circle of elms

we knew each other's names
and they never wavered
never struck
never dressed in rage

they whispered my true names
my land names
my wind names

they grew skin
like desert canyon walls

they sheltered nests
of baby mice in their roots

they stitched together
the marrow of my bones
threaded with the blood
of my Russian Cossack Grandfathers

who invaded
the Polish farms
of my Grandmothers

all escaped
across an ocean

into gang fights
knifings, and fur coats
in the Detroit bar they founded

but I seek the amnesty of trees
to feather my bones

indigenous of earth
my hands
open to the dark soil
the light full crystalline moon

my brothers stayed to wear
the two right shoes of righteousness

they see my branches
as enemy

but I was born to this land
I marry willows
and bear children each spring

I synthesize the sun into shelter
for all my relations
I bury the word them
in the earth

with the seeds
of other
until they sprout
as us

not woman
not poet
not crossed
not voter
not veiled
not stoned
not alone

we return sky spacious
indigenous cells
shared

not the few

but all

Dear Congress

I never want to hear the cries
the shattering bullets
from an automatic weapon
designed only to kill people
as fast as possible

so I'm sending you a pen

I want to read
in the local newspaper
how the 2nd grade-school kids
rescue a duckling
from a storm-drain

not cower quietly
under their desks

so I'm sending you a pen

I want to stop counting
flag-draped coffins
being unloaded
from Iraq, Afghanistan, Syria

so I'm sending you a pen

Dear Congress
there are children born
on this soil

to parents
that entered in the night
they need your shield
your lamps lit

so I'm sending you a pen

I want the name I choose
on the ballot
to be the one you count

to take the price tag off
the election

so I'm sending you a pen

I want my neighbors
to have access
to doctors and healers
without the fear of losing their homes

so I'm sending you a pen

I want laws that protect
our sky and oceans
more than the companies that leach
poisons and explode the shale
under our streets for oil

so I'm sending you a pen

Dear Congress,
I want to stand proudly beside you
as you use your courageous ink
to champion: We The People

so I'm sending you a pen

May our Poems

Rescue the homeless
    refugees caged
    by our own soldiers

Returning those stolen
    children back into the arms
    of their wailing families

May they melt the bars
    around the jailers
    and every suited policy-maker

May our poems explode gas-lights
    igniting the airwaves
    that fierce loyalty to profit/power

May our poems spark the revolution
    be the North Star
    draw maps into an equitable world

May our poems disarm
    the bloody bombs
    on parade down
    Pennsylvania Avenue

And the madman
    standing
    at salute

May our poems plant pussy willows
    and zinnia for the honeybees
    and songbirds
banning the pesticides
    that poison this world

May our poems
    mend away addiction
    become pain relievers

    nourishing
    those empty holes
    that never seem to fill

May our poems rip-off bandaids
    to expose every wound
    to the sunlight

May they be the balm
    the aloe and calendula
    that will finally heal us
    to the bone

Wage Sanity

Breathe in Congressional hearings and lying presidents
Breathe out free school lunches in Detroit and L.A.

Breathe in 6:00 am tweets from the Oval Office
Breathe out a poem's rhyming stanzas

Breathe in brown-skinned children in cages on our border
Breathe out a trip to your neighbor's house
with a basket of warm oatmeal cookies

Breathe in our National Parks left unprotected
Breathe out starry blankets under forever nights

Create sanity with a pen and notebook
and a Poet's fearless words

Think of the shy yellow tongues of Irises
instead of Rick Perry heading The Department of Energy

Wage sanity like a garden of snow-laden Dahlias
or a field of strawberries nestled on the land together

See the stars placed so carefully
in every creation story
and the sun that peaks
every morning

Weave sanity into your river of bones
like a circling eddy of calm tea in winter

Imagine all of the world's guns
melted into sculptures
and park benches

Plant maple trees that will blaze in the fall
for 200 years

Hug a stranger. Hug 5.
Look into each other's eyes
and smile

See this world now as awake

People holding open doors
and a place in traffic

Celebrate this tender world
as we see each other
beyond headlines and podium speeches

Hold open as many doors
as possible

In response to *"Wage Peace"* by Judyth Hill

Dear America,

can I call you mine? Do I belong in this melted pot this fiery cauldron where our brew is boiling over?

When will we elect a woman president? When will we value Ms. Cindy teaching our children how to read or Charles wrapped in his sleeping bag near the creek after work more than another bailout for Morgan Stanley or United Airlines?

Dear America, do I even look like you? I don't piss standing up. I don't wear high heels or lipstick or have Kaiser Insurance. I don't trust my safety to cops or generals or presidents. I wear a mask in public. I vote in every election and call congress but I don't seem to count.

I marched the day after the 2017 inauguration carrying a sign with a picture of Lady Liberty, crying. These days I say fuck a lot. I write poems, have a Lakota medicine wheel in my back yard and play my drum for the earth.

Dear America, when will we protect the fox crossing the road rather than saying she collaborated with the truck that flattened her?

When will we become the golden doorway for refugees, embracing the huddled, the wretched, the homeless? When will we refuse to build one more steel-barred wall along one more mile of border?

When will we quit polishing the medals? Make handguns easier to get than a free school lunch and then lament the violence?

When can I put my 9/11 poem away in the drawer?

America, can I call you that? It's arrogant since you're only a sliver between two oceans and we capitalize you as if this country is all that matters. And why do we believe we can carve our names over the graves, onto slices of soil and call it ours?

Even though my Grandmother's Grandmothers were born between two different oceans, my bones are your oaks, willows, and maple trees. I know the voices of grizzlies and coyotes and I feel the heartbeat of my Mother in this soil.

Dear America, you don't need to fold a flag over my grave even though I've marched against every one of your wars. One of your best kept secrets is that freedom really is free.

America, I am you. Are you me?

These Colors Don't run

If you could see
my fingers and both hands
you'd notice the shadowy stains
of amber-brown ink
embossing the lines deeper

I don't know why this ink
isn't labeled permanent
because in 3 washings
it still hasn't left my skin

but if this paper gets rain
on it even once
this color will run

I think of Vietnam war
veterans on Harley Davidsons
wearing American flag patches
with the words *These colors don't run*
and I used to know what that meant

now I'd like to make art
from that stained old flag
never added a star
for Puerto Rico
so no one cared

when she spun
under storms
under our factory storms

that destroy the sky
to make dollars
for a few

I'd like to build
a bonfire
offer up all
the colors
called country and
those bricks
that divide and
press conferences and
border prisons
and hungry children
and and and

and I want a pocket
filled with ands
some to hand out
and some
to remind myself
of the daily turnings
each small revolution
the pages I trust

I want to make
one-word to-do lists
and 50 word done lists

so I can find
those ands
that precede
every next

the ones that pray
a wood flute
sounds you can never hold
in your ink-stained hands

Borders are never ands
because you cannot build
bricks from breath

Words can be bricks
but the ands never stay
still long enough
to become mortar

Poets have super powers
because we write
between the bricks

little atom breaths
bouncing between
every etched line

Bomb 'em with butter
9/11/2001

I've been walkin through the world
counter spinning through the whirls
disagreeing with mass worth
I seek connection to the earth

I thought we'd found the real solution
in our conscious evolution
when along came the election
that ignored our selection

This seemed to take away our power
and to make the gentle cower
the old school that seemed so scary
that we thought we long had buried

in darkness once more rose
and in our hearts we froze
we're being asked to hold the truth
that's so apparent in our youth

We've a government hard to trust
that only values money's thrust
bringing us back to the dark ages
when other nations brought forth rages

and attacked our symbolic power
by destroying our twin towers
and our department of defense
trying to scare our government

now we're dividing our home nation
some say we've power of damnation
saying we can cure all evil
by killing even more people

But I say:
Bomb 'em with butter y'all
use your hearts and feed 'em all
if we meet their basic needs
then through love we'll plant the seeds

That the world is really one
our light all comes from the same sun
treat others as you wish to be
through listening we'll begin to see

that we're the keepers of the earth
that we're related through our birth
the One created all our relations
to come together as all nations
and be our common invocation

to hold one dream one thought of love
to honor each other and the ones above
to care for our mother our sacred earth
to care for our father who created our birth

Come on bomb 'em with butter fools
in honor of the golden rule
that peace begins within us all
that in this truth we must stand tall

Letter to COVID 19

If you have a plan
    keep it secret

Let us slow our feet
    as we leave driving
        to another day

Let us discover the colors
    in the eyes
        of a neighbor

and watch a stellar jay
    fight 2 sparrows
        as she adds grass to her nest

If you plan a body count
    don't let it spill

Let us count our seconds as unearned gifts
    wrapped in the spilled paint of sunrise
        and an evening's dusky stretch

If you have an expiration date
    don't write it on our calendars
        as we learn

to cook our meals slowly
    and linger at the wooden table

Let us silence the alarms
    that jolt us awake
        each morning

allowing our bodies to
    teach us their rhythm
        again

Let us discover
    smaller sheets of toilet paper

and closer letters
    in our last notebooks

Let us refill our fountain pens
    rather than tossing another
        empty cartridge

If you've come to change us
    let the soot-less air inhale a welcome
    as oil wells slow their
        frantic bowing

Let the children stalk black
    and amber caterpillars
        and the winter fur of cattails

Rather than sit straight in plastic chairs
    longing for the Spring air

A pandemic with Felix

Washing his face on the window sill
He deepens my morning, makes it still
His nose dark-wet from eating his fill
His purring soothes mountains into molehills

This pandemic— a lockdown, long stand-still
6 feet from each human, I hug him and chill
No matter what, his gaze says we will
Walk again with our friends, a new born thrill

Channeling Dr Seuss in a Quarantine

*What day could it be,
that is so remarkable you say?*
When last could you choose,
make it up this way?

Not since you were little
have you woke when you want
Decided on cooking
or carry from a restaurant

Go play with your kids,
take the dog for a walk
Just as long as you stay
6 feet away as you talk

Choose your own bedtime,
be your own boss
Notice these free days
are more profit than loss

We're all in this together,
shelter-in-place
Because we care about each other
we wait to embrace

So it's Friday before Saturday,
it's May before June
How do you want your days to be
when this lock-down ends soon?

"What day could it be, that is so remarkable you say?"
　　　Dr Seuss/The Cat in the Hat

　"it's Friday before Saturday, May before June"
　　　Wistawa Szymborska

ode to an eraser

not a censor
but soft
as silence

a pause
at the ready

contrails
of mystery

missing lines
on a page

the swoosh
of a wave
breaking
a prose sea

without wrestle
or wish

without ink

a dark felt
underbelly

cave in the center
compass point
indigo

eyes open
into the quiet

eraser
erasure
erase her

for the sake
of the poem

a little sadness
the body lost

the trust
free dive

Blue

    they tried to make us good
To color inside thick lines

    when we were already
Creating our own books

    ones where we knew
We were good

    whether or not we
Colored at all

    because why paste
Onto a page

    the changing sky
That infinite blue

    that we relegate
Into 4-letters–one word

    a border
A crayon

    too fat
For small fingers

    for the clouds
Frustrated depths

    we melt the crayon
Between our fingers

    to feel
What it means

    to be a sky

Letters to an Unknown God

I don't know where
to lift my eyes

I seek
the old ones
hewn from stone
cathedrals built
from shared crops
and worn fingers

I am forever drawn inside
those cold stone walls
the worn tiled mysteries
secret passages
no commoner
is allowed
to enter

as though we need secrets
on pages to initiate us
as though birth and souls
are not initiation enough

I search the inner highest point
surrounded in gold and turquoise
as a renaissance sky
for the pure white dove
with an olive branch
painted in the pinnacle

the angels with
the most battered wings
have worked the hardest
to intervene in our destruction

the pristine golden-winged ones
mostly keep to the other side
and sing the hallelujahs
of home coming
with a loftiness
I forget to believe in

teach me to love
and I will hand you my
ungloved fear

my knees were worn
at twelve years old
in a checkered skirt
in Catholic colors
and I cut a hole in the lower
left front and sewed on a patch
of two smiling orange mushrooms
and pleaded my case
by saying: *look, there was a hole!*

it was the independence I needed
a mushroom on the skirt
of the catholic poet
who wasn't allowed entry
and was born initiated
and always knew
those words

I carry the doves inside
my own cathedral
and only trust the ones
that trace a white
Holy Spirit in the domes

and still I don't know
who to pray to

to the dove in my heart?
to the ones who carry black leather
books with red silk page ribbons
in a language I was never taught?

do I trust my own battered wings
or sing to the golden ones
who always smile and wait?

and what does it matter
because when that moment comes
they WILL sing me home

this light
this light that sings itself

how do I pray to light?

battered or whole or gold or blue
how do I offer my
empty bank account
my empty bed
my own worn hands?

autographed by fire

at last night's bonfire
sober women in recovery

gathered around
sparking pallets

boards with rusted nails
a broken wagon wheel

flames
fueled with our offerings:

some old yearbooks
job resumes

fourth steps
boxes of prayers

a poem
to a deceased father

I held up my first edition
my author's copy of *Signs of Life*

the book cover
with the painted coyote skull

caressed in my hands
I gathered up my fear

of inadequate words
of revealing my story

of a too thin cover
80 pages of not-good-enough

printed and bound
and for sale

with my name on the front
one book existed

proof of nine years
of editing, writing, digging

1000's of words
and I tossed it

into the inferno
signing

the first copy
to God

The best poem I've written

today I woke up amazed

10,950 day-at-a-times

so much time spent pushing away
what's behind me now

and at this beautiful mountain view
it's about moving towards

10,950 day-at-a-times

learning to breathe
and having little choice but
to keep going, take the leap

15,768,000 minutes of
practiced *No, thank you's*
that have really been *yeses* in disguise

Today, I live.

I'm not in paper slippers
or a padded room, or staring
like a heart-pumping zombie

Today I show up to help a neighbor
in anxiety, picking up her crying child.

I answer the phone for a friend
who's afraid he may drink again.

Today no doctors measure my liver
and record the gross size
on my medical chart.

Today, I sing and write these words.
Miraculous, every one!

10,950 days without a hangover,
or trying to remember
who, what, where
or the night before

or how much money
will be in my wallet.

30 years of not always graceful
but usually grateful.

10,950 choices to know
where my feet are on the dance floor,

with no social-lubricants
or easy excuses for my behavior.

Sorry I was an ass, I was drunk
gets traded for:
Sorry I was an ass, I was … an ass

I was afraid
I was tired
I was human.
Please forgive me.

This poem is the best one so far,
by this woman who woke-up
on the day-after Christmas
as conscious as the-day-before.

No, 1-day more conscious
than the day-before
and the day-before.

10,950 choices
to suit-up and show-up

to feel and be awkward and amazing,
a human saying: *yes!*
to the messiness and miracles

to no-matter-what
the day brings.

I stand here naked at times
in the poem that hasn't ended
but only gets better and longer

Great Spirit is the editor
I'm still holding the pen
to a fresh-page
for another day

39 years ago I died.

And reluctantly returned.
A feet-in-cement-return.
A body with 5 toes in the grave pulling 1 out.
Only 1.
It felt so good to leave.
Why did the Doctor have to be so nice?
How did she have my last name on her lapel?
On her lips?
The married name I went by.
Why did she tell me her name over and over,
the invitation to offer mine back?
It's what polite people do. They trade names,
handles, monikers. It is the first intimacy. She was a
pesky fly in my face as I was out of this wet-suit body
and the meadows were so green. I was
weightless. My tethers slicing away.

And she kept telling me her name.
Until I recognized part of it as my own.
She kept telling me her name

How can a name create a miracle?
My own desire to respond?

How can all those strings to my own name
bring me back from the K in brink?

39 years ago today I died.
My forehead slumped onto my car horn,
making a thunderous blast.
7:00 a.m. outside of The Mountain Lion restaurant.
In a small mountain town.

And then someone told me her name.
Repeatedly.
Until I recognized my own.
How could she share my last name?

How did my head land?

Even then, angels.

Guardian Angel

Aiming for the sled hill
Eight years old frozen
Fields covered day
After Christmas
New tracks
5 foot sled
Enough for a family
Still sleeping
Alone a blue fuzzy
Coat, mittens, that broke
Dug-basement snow
Covered ice broke full
Water to the top under
The surface no water
Wings no one to hear
Broke my cries the
Surface broke soaked
Icy broke again
Grasped surface thin
My body
Broke heavier
When hands
Invisible held
Solid for enough
Moments for me
To fly

to heroin addiction

old windows gape
without reflection

absorbing
split-sliver nights

that stalk
32 years later

desperate as a
one-winged-bird

flying over

dwarf pines
needly

sliver moon
leaning

hollow-boned
familiar

red-brick
seductress

the haunting
abandon

draws me
still

Catalpa Tree/Sister

I worry
in May when the leaves
haven't arrived

June
when the fragrant
lotus-like
flowers fade

July when insects
munch holes
through the leaves

I pour enough water
into its roots

while you pour Rose
into your body

using alcohol to fertilize
turn away from the sun

as though the rays
might peel the bark
from your exposed skin

If you were the Catalpa
you wouldn't shake
in the morning

fall between
the sink and wall
when you try to stand

make promises of sobriety
you forget to keep

strip a person
bare with words
you can't take
back tomorrow

I have faith
in the Catalpa's
November-bare branches
their spiral reach

strong
through 80 mph gusts

their long bean-seeds
pointing to the ground

as though life is awake
even when asleep

and that you
are still worth
fighting for

Demons, again

I was encircled again
this morning

in the basement
of the house I'd built

the only way out
of that crowd

was to disintegrate
through the floor

leaving my deflated skin
a pile on the ground

I felt sad

you were the ones
I should have been able
to trust

today I unzipped your fur
to find trembling five-year-olds inside

I stepped over you

and flew

No Legacy

I used to share the stories
bone necklace on my throat

their burdens too constricting now
long years of volumes wrote

I toss their pages to the winds
and watch them as they float

trusting my remembering
to write me new, not rote

Shine

I have a cobalt-blue vase
    with running wolves
etched into the glass
    their elongated bodies

sprinting from carved
    cave walls
across modern meadows
    and ageless dreams

It holds 6 yellow Dahlias
    bravely doing what
they've always done

cupped petals absorbing
    the rhythm of Mother Earth

I give them enough water
    for their sun-heads
to express glory

but no crystal preservative
    to keep the stem-leaves green

It's asking too much
    to tear open the packet

stir in the powder
    with my wooden spoon

If I had children
>   their Cream of Wheat
would be lumpy

clothes a bit rumpled
>   tennies treadless

but we'd all have enough
>   to hold our heads high
and shine
.

Resilience

An amateur gardener told me that
petunias are old-ladies flowers
as I filled my front plot with their easy colors

their forgiving natures
of my inconsistent watering
and northern shade

Its hard to take them seriously
with names like petunia and pansy
sounding like panty and prissy and pink

But they ride close to the ground
and stay vibrant through October
if I do my part

I inhale purple/white striped bugles
royal-blues like melted crayons
reds the color of dragon hearts

I filled my flower box yesterday
and can see them from my kitchen
through my 64 year old windows

Sturdy and close to the ground

A Hallelujah (of waves)

perpetual ocean surf
tangled sea weed

surrendered bodies
woven strands

a court of royal cloud horses
tripping across the Gulf

web-tracks of sea gulls
the shape of kites

bucketfuls of children
digging quartz

crystal sand
into fortresses

child's silky toe prints
wet peach of sunset

soft coolings of evening
bathing away the news

shores sing praises
the tones of Angels

Orion's belt revealed
within a Milky ring

a hallelujah of waves
putting the day to rest

Appropriate

can a person
steal

an utterance?

A way
of touching
the earth?

The awe of gazing up
into the Pleiades

and falling to
one's knees,
to weep?

How can one
borrow a bell

vibrating ribs
encasing a heart

another
call to prayer?

Why should the nostrils
that inhale

chrysanthemums of lit sage
the liturgy of Frankincense
a wand of Nag Champa

turn away

if they did not first
absorb it
on Grandfather's breath?

Who hardcovers
certain lifted voices
into red-lined chapters
and cardinal laws?

Who are the
chosen ones

the margins
drawn on maps?

Which tree or bird or stone
gets to speak?

This world
is not quiet

to those who
have the privilege

to hear
to respond
to honor

this fabric
of belonging.

A conqueror's
bravado

musket voices
stormed

these shores
that no one saw
coming

the foreign fabric
no one could

no longer taught
the original ways.

Armored knees
steel plows

god doled out
piecemeal

with the punishment
of decrees

by those who
only journey
outward

misappropriate
war songs

construct
great walls

ownership

boots over
the earth

touching
the ground

only

in death

When to write a Prose Poem

When your fingers are too weary to ungrip the coffee mug

When you know the headlines will contain his name just as they have for 969 days

When you cannot find a sober relative

When you cannot remember the name of a friend

When the sky yellows, the wind an in-breath

When the red ant on your patio bites as deep as your bone and it still hurts 12 years later

When your carved cedar flute only plays one song

When you count your groceries in days

When you have to decide between new eyeglasses, superglue that's held for 2 years or x-raying a sore tooth

When the news steals your breath even before releasing the last one

When senators protect abusers and discredit whoever speaks truth

When you forget the words to Bob Dylan's
Blowing in the Wind

When you sit down one morning to write your dreams and find they have been erased

When poetry is the only voice you trust, it is time.

reluctant power animal
(of our current president)

I see a caged molting parrot
kissing his smudged mirror

whistling and tweeting
Bad hombres, build a wall

or a smelt fish swimming in circles
following silver flashes around and around

a howling monkey at dusk
terrorizing the dreams of villagers

a no-see-um
leaving itchy little welts
that no one knows
where they came from

a baboon thumping his orange chest
roaring alone in the jungle

maybe his power animal is a
trained flea/circus ring-master

or a miller moth
annoying mobster
that can't stay away from the fire

Untolled

a rusted
temple bell
a rotted
hanging cord

a missing
wood clapper

That's what
this presidency
is like

I could circle
a length
of flax cord
through the top ring

string it onto
a low branch
of the Catalpa tree
behind my house

But
it would hang silent
its tongue shocked loose
the November before last
when the election machines
turned rogue

A bell
without a voice
is like a body
without a heart
a drum
with a split skin
a country
led by the enemy

This bell
can only speak
in rusted Braille

can only echo
what once was

Ring

silver curve, shaped
around my finger

there's a split where
you were joined

I expected to fail
30 years ago, maybe 34

when I split from
my own wars

I received you because
your story also ached

your first guardian
left his blood

in Viet Nam
now we survive together

sixteen odd chips of turquoise
from sixteen mines

on this land I love
sixteen colors of grass into sky

into clear, sober eyes
sixteen waves of lifetimes

one birth
sixteen muses

and I find irresistible beauty in each
nestled into sixteen silver squares

of breath, of open
sixteen passions pin-balling around

a bingo board of numbers called
on any given day

companion
sixteen stories assembled

an artists care
in the old way

when that was the way
sixteen stone stories

to pass on to a niece
when story is all

that is left of me
sixteen stories

crafted smooth
in the old way

Touch

I startled you when
I touched your arm
through the ragged blanket

your life
compacted cardboard

a 4' x 7' cubicle
on the corner of
Sarasota and Light Street

a broom for the Baltimore sidewalk
bungeed tight against your wall

blended in to the cold
in to the dark

not even bothering
to ask

anymore

brother

my brother

I worry about you

sometimes
I believe

a little can
make a difference

maybe three years ago
maybe eight

a few coins could've gotten
you into tomorrow

today there is no
next day

today there is not even
another blanket

today there is not
another word that matters

7 Degrees

some cities look
better from the air

planes unbroken
by rust colored
sleeping bags

patchwork quilts
under bridges

I thought
7 degrees
was cold

I cannot turn
my face
towards the wind

one tear
from my left eye

knowing a few dollars
won't make a ripple

to the lone woman
rocking in the alcove

I placed $10 into your mittened hands
on my way to the convention center
under the overpass

you met my eyes, pulled the
pink wooly scarf
from around your mouth

told me I didn't need to
give you my money

told me you have money
and didn't need more

I asked, *Mama, what are you doing
out here in the freezing cold?*

you relied: *I'm homeless!*
I asked about a shelter
you said they're too crowded

I hugged her tight
Told her I didn't like
her being out there

I kissed her
on top of her hat

said I loved her
and she said it back

I left her rocking
on the marble ledge

I left her rocking

I left her rocking

I left her

In the Shape of Mourning
For Pulse Nightclub / Orlando – June 12, 2016

>Make this poem
>in the shape
>of an IV bag
>
>dancing
>Pulsing kids
>
>750 bullets
>per minute
>
>one finger
>one trigger
>one time
>
>and hold...
>
>Write this poem
>in the shape
>of mourning
>
>not the one
>the clock pilots
>but the one
>the sun
>doesn't rise
>upon

Write this poem
in the shape
of two rainbows

that split the sky
into thirds yesterday

the sky that grieved
tears and
the sun
that struck
them
beautiful

Make this poem
in the shape of
all that isn't holy
isn't of God

at 750 bullets
per minute

But know
the holiness
of shattered
rainbows

and the holiness
of rain

This Winter's Day
For Mary Oliver

a full quorum of snow
covers my backyard
in the color it should be
in January

reclaiming the brown
winter-dormant grass
that drones a longing
into the back of my mind

I write this tribute poem
on the day after your passing

and it seems
it should be snowing
the sun bowing homage
while it reads your poems

allowing you to be
the one to shine today

You, of course,
would give the clouds
center stage

that slow us into
a deeper rhythm
for this one day,
this one wild and precious day

*in this one wild
and precious life*

You would take time
to count crows
and weave ibis wings
upon your tongue

seeking prayers
in a blade of grass
beneath a broken bottle
in an abandoned city lot

your knees knowing the soil
and the winds, your voice

and for so many of us,
your precious words

wild and free

Tell me, what is it you plan to do / with your one wild and precious life?"
Mary Oliver *The Summer Day*

The Journey
For Mary Oliver

6 mornings
past your flesh

emptying
your poetry

leaving the pages
our inheritance

leaving us richer
than when you found us

but you didn't find us

you deeply found
yourself

in blades of Sea Grass
wing feathers of wild geese

you lived slow
amongst the trees

and described
the ache

each exhaled breath
unpainting

each inhale's
prison-grey

you wrote through
flawed ancestral blood

echoes
of unwanted hands

you wrote into
the real journeys

your own soft belly
refusing penance

Sky Bled Red
For Pamelita Joy

fuchsia tears
running down
the painting

spraying
with a mist bottle

to not stop
dripping
oozing
bleeding

not yet done
grieving

wet paper swells
the painting propped
so the colors fall

from the sky
through the arms
of a Spirit tree

that caught your

hurtling body
burning motorcycle
tossed soul

propelled into its branches
till you were ready
tears were dry

till you saw
your crimson body

fiery
Road King
held

an offering

For Jim (the man of) Steele

You were walking
your beat
that night

a bevy of poems
on your shoulder

new ones
in your mind

honing a Poet's
attention

the cool air
on your cheek

Blake Street lights
feathering the lines

walking
from one gig
to the next

never reading
a poem
the same way
twice

you tempted
the devil

at the crossroads

looked him
in the eye

threw down verses
a pulpit preacher

You put rhythm
to injustice

and justice
into rhyme

weighing every
fire-lit word

Jimmy
your voice

will never

be silenced

every Front
Range Poet

carries
a few notes

of you
in them

like blood

only better

What isn't in (your) poem

   the Toyota
      red
   the way your body
      red
   if your shoes were
      tied
   if your poems
      flew
   if you never
      saw
   if the driver
      heard
   poems or the
      sounds
   of sirens
      or the
   crush of
      you
   empty cap on
      the street
   how you waited
      your turn
   how many other cars
      injured
   your body
      uncaged
   the way I always
      knew you

Don't stay home

The morning nudges
my shoulder, tells me

don't look
for what you lost
yesterday

yesterday's longings
are bed sheets,
sweaty and tattered

and today
is born
into dawn

it was all a dream, she says
empty, vanished, nothing
to go looking for

your loves are
the eyelashes
that feather
this day

the beauty
that frames
your sight

do not stay home
the thick night
that looks

like the night before
and the night before

greet, she tells me
go find a new day

There's no Place

Dorothy's house
once again caught wing

yet this time
there's no wickedness
to soften her landing

the clouds intervened
and azure dreams

wove a net
so thick

blue bells and tulips
had to stretch
their necks

to reach the light

seeds
blew up like kites
racing the sun

to greet this girl
who learned

that home
is everywhere

how to write an erotic poem
(in a crowded coffee shop)

purchase an apple
a sweet crisp Fuji

slowly peel the white
oval, sticky barcode

lightly scratch her hips
with your nails

stroke her brown, protruding
stem with your thumb
and forefinger

squeeze, twist it
into a slow release

caress her flushed pink
skin with your fingers, palms
trace her curves

spread your mouth
around her firm
succulent body

feel the pulse
the seeds deep within

allow your teeth to sink in
moan from your chest

move through her
glistening flesh

her juices linger
sweet flavors spread

awaken to erect
the cilia on your tongue

body tingling
craving more

move lustily past
her wet flesh

back to her skin
polished with life

thrust your teeth in again
devouring her

imagine her as Eve
temptation

if you eat of this knowledge
there will be no return

banishment
the old garden

but to never
taste anything
so fully
deeply

flesh of the stars
soul of the moon

the serpent beckons
rises

undulates, shimmers
with the musty smell
of fresh earth

her core breached
seeds
a new pleasure

heaven etching marriages
inside your skin

fingers making a new language
each stagger of breath

your arms, lungs
your legs pulsate

each panting grasp for air
paint the sky

a spiral dance
beyond the planets

you reach for more of her
the earth becomes too small

falling back to genesis
to the chapters before words

where serpents turn
inside-out

you push her away

afraid of your own skin

Never before written

there are not enough metaphors
to trace

your skin
your thighs

a collage
of us

I inscribe
you

into a 14 line sonnet
my breath punctuating

vellum pages stripped into
soaked wet pleases

I enter this Nile
your life-giving river

reflected by the Milky Way
and am lost

I reach for the mountains
and I name the stars

my hands dive through chapters
your ocean

verses of language
only cried in ecstasy

each stroke of your fingers
an iambic beat

arching my back
into rhyme

mixed tears of release
pulsing/every pore

an impossible
alliteration

breath
seeking home

finding meter
finding rippled rhythm

the ellipsis
a whole new universe

the womb
a whole new Goddess

I talk in tongues
trace my words

in a spiral
my mouth

everywhere
not dry

your verse is epic
and devours me

never before written

captured on a page

I spread everything
before you

I always trust
the poem

Heckle / Jeckle

Disney
was our dream-weaver

who taught us
the world is a golden castle

raven's caws
are the cackles of magpies

crickets
wisdom keepers in top hats

Uncle Walt wove us into tales
with a hypnotic voice

wide-eyed children
thirsty to reach the sun
the stars
fairies
princesses

blue birds landing
on our shoulders

as we emerged
from lime green kitchens

hungry for the world's feast
in languages we did not yet

I ventured
wrapped in invisible wings

into the unlit streets
the burned-out buildings

lost in the maze
of Detroit

stopping to ask
three men on a wire

the safe way home

and
true to life

they always pointed
the wrong way

crow courage

they came
thick, dark cloud

seven o'clock everyday
they soldiered

overhead
to the gathering

tree raucous
laden in black

plans drawn
reports given

orders cawed
loud agreement

seven o'clock
drum circle

signaled in
faithfully

a feather
of support

black prayer
left daily

on my doorstep
to help me

take
my medicine

High Water Sonata

you play the flood

on your guitar

rain tapping

up the frets

all ten fingers pound

unstoppable chords

punctured sky empties

sliding prairie dogs

into rivers, fish into

walls - propane tanks

downstream

muddy surge axing

through kitchen windows

sand cemented into

closets, carpets

staccato drops

swallowing land fast

hands tearing through

ghosts of missing bridges

concrete buckles

new notes

under your hands

Your song slows

drained sky abandons

sun teased back in

string by string

Dark Moon

new moon gathers
light from within

through long
dreamy nights

following the council
of planets

weaving new poems
a sacred waltz

somersaults of
Orion

tea spilling from
the Little Dipper

every star a guide
new constellations

each season
each year of a life

letting go
of everything

resting
without burdens

long dark nights
allies

a Crone's silver
braids

I open my window

when the moon is close
and round

even when the light
is not on my side

I hope to catch
a few octaves

strumming the keys
of Andromeda

waltz along
a scattered alphabet

stars of
drifting letters

before words
before absolutes

this intoxication
of possibilities

every star a guide
new constellations

each season
each year of a life

letting go
of everything

resting
without burdens

long dark nights
allies

a Crone's silver
braids

I open my window

when the moon is close
and round

even when the light
is not on my side

I hope to catch
a few octaves

strumming the keys
of Andromeda

waltz along
a scattered alphabet

stars of
drifting letters

before words
before absolutes

this intoxication
of possibilities

Autumn

When you fall
on the white soft lace
of moth wings

drunk from long fiery days
soaring now
towards a silver moon

You will know
the star/web/sky
as you move into
dream time

When you fall
your willow-trunk full
of summer's marriage vows

thunder-filled rain
the lightnings of childhood

You will release pages
of leaves
stories
read and absorbed

You will become the tome
shedding into new paradigms
not yet written

in new languages
not yet dreamt

When you fall
it will be on scented apples
and purple plums

a chorus of crickets
singing the earth's songs

Crisp leaves clattering
a rhythm section
under the wind's breath

When you fall
you will gain your feet
on the granite of earth

You will release the need
to hold up anymore

trusting the arms of this season
to catch you

to read you the poems
you began writing
on the day of your first breath

Listen

Aspen trees
unclothed Maples

whispering your names
back to you

Related

I am St Francis of Assisi
and I am the long-night's chant
I am the over-burdened burro
and the prayer for forgiveness at death

I am the first star I called forth councils
and I am the tribes that appeared
I am Saturn's rings that spin
and the jade dust that color them green

I am the lead in the Alchemist's room
and I am the formula for gold
I am the rawhide rattle and the drumbeat of mothers
and the ceremonialist who weaves it in prayer

I am the bone blade and I am the altar
I am the flute the magic the maker
I am the dancer the weaver the poet
I am the teacher the student the crone

I am the crimson mums in autumn
and I am the naked tree
I am the rust-colored moth seeking the sun in October
and I am the bear that feeds
I am the Shaman that rises up
and I am the ground that sleeps

Christmas Cactus

Shy buds measure the sunlight
emerging on Thanksgiving week
to announce the Holy Days

Ancient friend
doesn't follow impeachments
or border walls

marking time
in the way
its supposed to be marked

from a child's budding
through a life's exuberance
into the shriveling fuchsia

when it's time to let go
gratitude
for all that beauty

Its how we change the world
one blooming conversation
overflowing a clay pot

a new green limb
committed to showing up
no matter what

every reach
an imprint
for how we love

Still Point
(Winter Solstice)

Hush
Can you feel it?
A stillness over the land

Our northern hemisphere
The colors of dreams and sleeping fields
Owls blessing the shadows

The long nights lit by star-maps
Orion lets his arrows fly
Lighting the way

The angels closer
To your ear
While you dream

Each cell, each planet within
Resting winter's earth

Renewing before
The sun's return

Be still
And know

My stone bear closed one eye this December

actually tossed free
one round turquoise bead
she's peered through
for 16 years

we're alike that way

I often chose
not looking
as my tool

If I knew
where the blue bead ended up
I'd glue her back together

but maybe wait
past winter solstice

past a good deep
hibernation

when she'd feel
like opening them again

I like the option
of being able to soften
my vision

remove my glasses
not have everything
so cuttingly clear
as the harsh north wind

Like painting snow and Evergreens
in the colors I feel
rather than the way they look

or crafting a poem
the way I hear it
rather than the way
it was said

It's time to read past
glaring headlines
and an inaugural throne

see the moments as holy
and our future in the sun's return

Holiday lights soften
the pine needles
on dark, long nights

tinsel reflects like
rainbows of ice
and a stillness is born

away from crowded inns
where people gather
to avoid their loneliness

I don't need my eyes now
but the vision of sages

who navigate by star light
and bring gifts

for all of us
by right of being born

the shelter of gold
healing of frankincense
and clarity of myrrh

I don't like my stone bear
only having one eye

I turn her towards
the wall to rest

see what emerges
come spring

I know
she will emerge

with the brightening days
that always brighten

and for now
I get to rest, too

Amazing Grace Revisited

Amazing Grace
how sweet the sound
that calls us to our knees
in beauty's face
and beauty's song
it's beauty sets us free

Amazing Grace
how sweet the sound
that gifts sobriety
I once was lost
but now am found
was trapped and now I'm free

Amazing Grace
the sun and stars
the moon that tames the sea
this earthly plane
we've traveled far
to find your love and peace

Amazing Grace
how sweet the sound
that calls us to our knees
in beauty's face
and beauty's song
it's beauty sets us free

8 days

its taken
this long
to arrive

anywhere my
skin is

its taken
the decision
to leave

to finally
get here

Remember me this way

a holy perch
of ravens
watch from
a craggy
cathedral

vertical
prayers chanted
into crimson
sandstone cliffs

I rest my bones
onto soft
warm earth

a breeze
wakes my skin

a man
in a uniform
shines his police car
in the lot behind me

the sounds of
pow-wow drumming
emanates from
his car radio

the door slams
wheels crunch gravel
under sparkling rims
taking away the songs

leaving only the quiet
and myself

I soar
on raven wings
to the mountain
whose pines I smell
from a mile away

the cardinal stones
chant my name

embrace the drum
of my heart

they always
call me back

words
carved into
temples
drum beats
chanting heart

the shiny rules
that leave me
to silence

remember
me
this
way

Obituary for a Poet

She kept folding time
back onto
itself

a long-form
poem

wild rhymes
that deepened

creating birth
no birth
rebirth

aging
in reverse

writing the poem
backwards

bottom
to top

till no one
knew

how old
she was

till slowly
she disappeared

into
ink

ACKNOWLEDGMENTS

Letters to an Unknown God won the National Federation of State Poet Societies' Winners Circle Award 2016 and was published in *Encore 2016*, a collection of prize winners

This Winter's Day won the Colorado Author's League Best Poem Award 2020

Resilience won *Honorable Mention* in *The Columbine Poet's Society* contest 2019

This Winter's Day was published by The Colorado Independent Newspaper online in the *News Poetry* section

Dear Congress was published by The Colorado Independent Newspaper online in the *News Poetry* section

Crow Courage and *Bomb em with Butter* were previously published in my chapbook: 13 *Moons on Turtle's Back*

GRATITUDES

To the incredible community of poets who teach and inspire me, break open my heart, name the unnamable, light the lamps in darkness, who create their art and speak true, especially when its hard. You have given me space to find my voice, my way, by holding open doors and being true to yourselves.

    A special thank you to Anne Waldman and The Jack Kerouac School of Disembodied Poetics, SETH, Julie Cummings, Anita Jepson-Gilbert and The Columbine Poets, The Mercury Cafe, Ziggies Poetry Festival, NFSPS, the Western Slope Poets, all of the open mikes and reading series, my editor Max Regan, and my friend and fellow performer Cathy Casper. A special thank you to Kika Dorsey, MD Friedman, Lorrie Wolfe and Dorothy Walters. You have all contributed in ways I cannot begin to measure and have helped me become the poet and woman I am today.

ABOUT THE AUTHOR

VALERIE A SZAREK grew up around Detroit, Michigan, exploring the woods, playing her wood flutes for the full moon and elms, and marching on The Detroit Tank Arsenal against the Vietnam War. Friends say they never saw her without a notebook or sketchbook in hand. Except for Art and English, she skipped a lot of classes in high school to sit in a quiet hallway or bathroom floor, reading Alan Watts, Eric Fromm, and Hermann Hesse. At 19 years old she founded Breezy Lady Leather (later Breezy Mountain Leather), a custom leather shop. This business thrives today in her home in Louisville, Colorado.

Valerie says she became a Poet the week of 9/11 when she received the words to *Bomb em with Butter* and wrote them down as though taking dictation. She read it to anyone who would listen and found her light through the tunnel, through life with this poem, and the ones that have followed. She sees Poet as her way in the world and shares this heart-centered invitation to see, hear, and honor each other wherever she goes. The IRS agent, Comcast customer service, the washing machine salesman, deli clerk and doctor all know her poems.

She is an award winning performance Poet, being named the Blissfest Poet of the Year in 2018. She's won a Colorado Author's League first place Award, a National

Poetry Federation first place Winner's Circle Award, and an EVVY Award. She performed at the International Young People's Conference and has been a feature at many Colorado festivals.

She teaches soul-centered writer's workshops, is a Shamanic and Energy healer (offering long-distance and in-person sessions), a Native American Flute player, drummer, Ceremonialist, and leather artisan.

Website: poetval.com
Email: val@poetval.com

www.ingramcontent.com/pod-product-compliance
Lightning Source LLC
Chambersburg PA
CBHW060402080526
44583CB00012B/439